CHAUCER

AND HIS WORLD

An ampulla for oil or holy water from Canterbury, a pilgrim's souvenir of a visit to the shrine of Thomas à Becket, which was noted for its healing powers.

The Wilton Diptych, an exquisite fourteenth-century altarpiece, displays the magnificence of a medieval king, as the young Richard II, attended by patron saints, adores the Virgin and Child.

CHAUCER
AND HIS WORLD

IAN SERRAILLIER

LUTTERWORTH PRESS · LONDON

First published 1967

TO JANE

Acknowledgements

THE Author has consulted the following sources in the preparation of this book: *A Reader's Guide to Chaucer* by Muriel Bowden (Thames and Hudson), *Chaucer in his Time* by Derek Brewer (Nelson), *Notes on Chaucer's Prologue*, English Literature series, by W. Carpenter-Jacobs (Common Ground), *A History of the English-Speaking Peoples* by Winston Churchill (Cassell), *Chaucer: The Canterbury Tales* translated into modern English by Nevill Coghill (Penguin), *Chaucer and his England* by G. G. Coulton (Methuen), *The Age of Chaucer* edited by Boris Ford (Pelican), *English Wayfaring Life in the Middle Ages* by J. J. Jusserand, *Nine Days' Hero: Wat Tyler* by Jack Lindsay, *England in the Late Middle Ages* by A. R. Myers (Pelican), *A History of Everyday Things in England* by Marjorie and C. H. B. Quennell (Batsford), *The Complete Works of Geoffrey Chaucer* edited by F. N. Robinson (Oxford), *Chaucer: The Prologue to the Canterbury Tales* edited by W. W. Skeat (Oxford), and *Illustrated English Social History: I* by G. M. Trevelyan.

The translations from *The Canterbury Tales* are by the author, with the exception of those on pages 22 and 32 which are taken from Nevill Coghill's translation by kind permission of Penguin Books Ltd.

The publishers wish to thank the following for permission to reproduce photographs of which they hold the copyright. The numbers in brackets refer to the pages on which they appear: Aerofilms Ltd. [13 (upper), 20]; Bibliothèque Nationale, Paris [8]; Bodleian Library, MS Bodl. 264, ff. 91r, 79 [29 (upper), 38 (upper)]; British Museum [5, 11 (upper), 12, 13 (lower), 15 (lower), 16 (lower), 21, 22, 23 (right), 24 (left), 25, 29 (lower), 31 (left), 32, 33, 36 (right), 42 (upper), 44, 46 (upper)]; Central Office of Information [30 (upper)]; Corpus Christi College, Cambridge [47]; Essex Record Office [14 (upper)]; the Burrell Collection, Glasgow Art Gallery and Museum [28 (lower), 43 (upper)]; Guildhall Museum [1, 28 (upper), 35 (lower), 37 (lower), 38 (lower)]; Henry E. Huntington Library and Art Gallery [23 (left), 48]; London Museum [15 (upper), 17, 18 (upper), 31 (right), 36 (left)]; Ministry of Public Building and Works [10, 40 (lower), 41 (upper right and lower left)]; Museum of Leathercraft [18 (upper right), 34]; National Buildings Record [16 (upper), 30 (lower), 35 (upper), 45]; the Trustees of the National Gallery [2]; National Maritime Museum [43 (lower)]; Nationalmuseum, Copenhagen [18 (lower)]; National Portrait Gallery [39 (lower)]; R. Ewart Oakeshott [41 (lower right)]; Picturepoint Ltd. [37 (upper)]; the Controller of H.M. Stationery Office for Crown Copyright documents (E101/393/11, f. 70, E207/6/2, no. 56) in the Public Record Office [7, 9 (lower)]; Royal Commission on Historical Monuments [11 (lower), 26, 27]; Studio Briggs [42 (lower)]; Trinity College, Cambridge [19 (upper left)]; Victoria and Albert Museum [18 (lower)]; the Trustees of the Wallace Collection [14 (lower), 40 (upper), 41 (upper centre)]; War Office [39 (upper)]; the Dean and Chapter of Westminster Abbey [24 (right)]; Whipple Science Museum [9 (upper)]. The Publishers are most grateful to Miss Mary Remnant for allowing her rebec [46 (lower)] to be photographed for this book.

Printed in Great Britain
by The Camelot Press Ltd.,
London and Southampton

Geoffrey Chaucer. A portrait commissioned soon after his death by an admiring Thomas Hoccleve (1370?–1450?), who wished to preserve Chaucer's likeness for all time.

THE EXACT date of Geoffrey Chaucer's birth is not known, but it was probably somewhere between 1340 and 1345. His mother is believed to have been Agnes de Copton, and the name of his father was John. They lived in London, in Thames Street, by the busy waterway and port, and not far from the Tower of London. John Chaucer was a vintner. His family belonged to the prosperous middle class and had been in the wine trade for several generations.

The boy was brought up in the cosmopolitan society of trade, with its firm links with France. He would have been taught to read before he went to school—perhaps by a clerk in lower orders anxious to add to his slender income. There were three grammar schools in London, and he was probably sent to the one nearest his home, St. Paul's Almonry. Here Latin was the principal subject taught. French he would have picked up at home and among the merchant vintners, in addition to what he learnt at school. The upper and middle classes all spoke French. Religion, reading, arithmetic and possibly some natural science were also on the curriculum.

In 1357 he went off to be a page in the household of the Duchess of Ulster. She was the wife of Prince Lionel, third son of King Edward III. Here he remained till some time between 1363 and 1368, the year of Prince Lionel's death. In this position he must have waited on the most important people in the land and had the best possible opportunity to observe good manners as well as character. He came into contact with courtiers and statesmen, soldiers and ambassadors, artists, musicians, craftsmen, merchants, lawyers, doctors, churchmen. His duties included making beds, holding and carrying torches, and taking messages for the chamberlain. At night he slept on the floor of the great hall. When after five years he was promoted to squire, he was allowed to share a small room and a servant with a fellow squire, and his wages rose to $7\frac{1}{2}$*d.* a day. We do not know when he started writing poems, but his *The Book of the Duchess* (1369) reflects the experience of this period of his life. No doubt he was writing experimentally, for penning verses to a lady love, as well as drawing and composing music, were common accomplishments for a squire. The Squire in the Prologue to *The Canterbury Tales* is no exception:

> Poet he was, composer, and, what's more,
> Could dance, joust in the lists and write and draw.

In 1359 Chaucer was sent abroad to fight the French in what is now called the Hundred Years' War. He was still a squire (roughly the equivalent of a second lieutenant in the modern army) and never rose to the higher rank of knight. That winter he was taken prisoner near Rheims. The following year he was ransomed for £16 (perhaps £1,600 in modern money) and went home. Probably he lacked the temperament for soldiering, but there were other ways in which he could be useful to the Crown. Clearly King Edward III thought highly of him, for he contributed part of the ransom himself.

In 1366 or thereabouts he married Philippa de Roet, lady-in-waiting to the Queen and sister of John of Gaunt's third wife. John of Gaunt was Duke of Lancaster and son of King Edward III. Love played little part in a medieval marriage, and it is doubtful if in this union Chaucer found any true companionship. Marriages were usually arranged by parents or friends, and in high society child marriages were all too frequent. The French Princess Isabella was only seven when she was married to King Richard II, who came to the throne in 1377 at the age of eleven and died in 1399. Chaucer does not address any poems to his wife or ever refer to her directly. His allusions to married life are mostly ironical and seldom flattering. Although at that time a wife was expected to defer to her husband and obey him, the ebullient Wife of Bath in *The Canterbury Tales* could hardly be said to conform to this pattern.

In 1373, five years after Prince Lionel's death, Chaucer was sent to Italy for the first time—he was to return again in 1378—on the King's business. What this business was is not known; it was probably a trade mission. But the visit had a tremendous effect on his development as a poet. It brought him into close contact with what was then the finest art and literature in the world. The Gothic architecture of Pisa, Florence and Genoa was fresh and new. Giotto had died only recently, and painting and sculpture were flourishing. Dante, to whose style he owes so much, had died in 1321. But Petrarch and Boccaccio, the greatest contemporary European writers, from whose poems and

A page from King Edward III's accounts recording the payment of sixteen pounds for the ransoming of "Galfrid(us)" Chaucer (the entry begins at the end of the fourth line). The accounts were kept in Latin with set abbreviations for frequently recurring words.

de Suffolke Iohanni Forster et Iohanni de Chastres contilibus (?) licenciatis ad partes
suas propria curie contra xij li. de consilio dono Regis die et anno supradictis
xxxvj li. Roberto Salman Willelmo Hengstman et Iohanni Smyth
curie contra xvj s. de consilio dono Regis eodem die et anno xlviij. Galfrido
Chaundeler capto per inimicos in partibus Francie in subsidium redempcionis sue de consilio
dono Regis die et anno supradictis xvj li. Domino Iohanni de Swylton
militi Burgundie misso per Regem Francie pro Angliae de consilio dono Regis
xvj li. Reginaldo Heraldo armorum commorante cum Rege de partibus Germanie
de consilio dono Regis iiij li. Iohanni Thorlbode et Thome de Chestre valettis
capto per inimicos in subsidium redempcionis sue de consilio dono Regis lxj s. Iohanni
de Massingham et valettis sub ipso existentibus reparantibus pontem de Sheen de
consilio dono Regis iiij li. Domino Iohanni de Beyle in subsidium unius equi
sibi emendi de consilio dono Regis tercio die Februarii xx li. Domino Roberto
de Clinton pro uno equo sibi emendo de consilio dono Regis tercio die Marcii
anno supradicto xvj li. xiij s. iiij d. Ricardo le Fissher in subsidium unius equi
sibi emendi de consilio dono Regis xl s. Iohanni Samdonell misso per Regem
Avinion de consilio dono Regis c s. Magistro Iordano phisico in subsidium
unius equi sibi emendi de consilio dono Regis iiij li. Iohanni de Wyryngton
Waltero Albyn et Waltero Maghan curie contra c s. in subsidium unius equi sibi
emendi de consilio dono Regis xx li. Domino Michaeli Coskyn licenciato ad partes
proprias de consilio dono Regis xvj li. xiij s. iiij d. Henrico de Whitbergh cum lit.
ad partes proprias de consilio dono Regis octavo die Aprilis anno supradicto xx li. Willelmo
Godknape palefridario Regis Waltero Courtmaine Willelmo Ferrere et Roberto atte Crosse
captis per inimicos in subsidium redempcionis sue viij die Aprilis de consilio
dono Regis anno supradicto xvj li. Galfrido Hakkyngton et Thome de Wellowe
valettis domine Regine curie capto per inimicos in subsidium expensarum suarum versus
curiam viij li. de consilio dono Regis xvj li. Domino Ricardo Burgoyne licenciato
ad partes suas proprias de consilio dono Regis xl li. Willelmo de Mountagu
valetto Abbatis de Mountagu de consilio dono Regis xxiij s. Ricardo
Fissher in subsidium unius equi sibi emendi de consilio dono Regis lx s.
Domino Roberto de Thorpe licenciato ad partes proprias de consilio dono Regis anno
supradicto xij li. Willelmo Loughlere et Iohanni Fyge valettis Regis in subsidium
expensarum suarum versus curiam iiij li. de consilio dono Regis anno supradicto
viij li. Willelmo Gilber valetto domini Iacobi de Sudbury commoranti
cum Rege de partibus Anglie cum ... de consilio dono
Regis anno supradicto x li. Iohanni Valletto capitali de
St. Michaele in subsidium expensarum suarum de consilio dono Regis [illegible]
Iohanni de Wodestok garcioni garderobe in subsidium expensarum
suarum de consilio dono Regis anno supradicto xx s.

Summa istius pagine ... mcccviij li. vj s. viij d. ...

... viij li. ... viij d. ...

The French king, Charles V, receiving ambassadors. Chaucer served as a member of a royal embassy on several occasions and visited Charles V's court.

stories he borrowed so freely, were still alive, and he may even have met them.

On his return to London in 1374 he was made Controller of Customs on wools, skins and hides in the Port of London, a post he held till 1386. During this time he went abroad several times on the King's business, to France, Flanders and Italy. From the King he received the grant of a pitcher of wine daily for life, from John of Gaunt a life-pension, and from the Corporation of the City of London the lease of the house over Aldgate gate, where he remained till at least 1385. It was probably the happiest period of his life; his post was not too burdensome and he had more time for study than he had ever had at court. He translated Boethius, the Roman philosopher and historian. Working from French, Latin and Italian sources, he wrote *Troilus and Criseyde* (*c.* 1372–84), a romantic poem in rhyme royal in five books, sometimes called the first novel in English, and one of his finest achievements. It introduced to England the new Italian style and the first breath of the Renaissance. In the fashionable French medieval style he wrote *The Parliament of Fowls* (*c.* 1377–82), a St. Valentine's Day poem, with birds indulging in sprightly and dramatic conversations, *The House of Fame* (1379), a very funny dream fantasy, and *The Legend of Good Women* (1384–6), tales about women such as Cleopatra, Dido and Ariadne, who were faithful in their love until death. It has a witty and charming prologue and was the first poem in English to use the heroic couplet, which was later to become one of the most popular of all verse forms. Poet, diplomat and man of business, Chaucer was now a figure of position and affluence. In 1386 he was made a Justice of the Peace and elected to Parliament as Knight of the Shire of Kent.

The same year his good fortune changed. His patron, John of Gaunt, was sent on a military expedition to Spain and replaced at Richard II's court by the Duke of Gloucester. Chaucer lost all his offices. Perhaps the blow may now be regarded as a blessing in disguise, for it gave him the leisure to start on the greatest of his poems, *The Canterbury Tales.*

Even so, his public career was not yet over. In 1389 John of Gaunt returned to favour, and the young king appointed Chaucer Clerk of the Works. He was given charge of the maintenance of the Palace of Westminster, the Tower of London, St. George's Chapel, Windsor, Berkhamstead Castle, and a number of royal residences, as well as of all the walls, ditches, drains and bridges between Greenwich and Woolwich. Perhaps he was inefficient in his duties, for he lost the Clerkship in 1391 and not, as far as we can see, for political reasons.

From now till the end of his life, in spite of an increase in his pension, his financial position was never really secure. His wife had died some years earlier, when their son "little Lowis" was still a child. His last poems tell of the sadness of growing old, of the loss of poetic powers, of illness and disillusionment, though he seems to have met these blows with courage and acceptance. He never finished *The Canterbury Tales.* On October 25, 1400, he died at the house he leased in the grounds of Westminster Abbey. His tomb in the Abbey was the first of those which are grouped together in Poets' Corner.

An astrolabe, a scientific instrument used for making astronomical observations in order to establish, among other things, the correct time and the longitude and latitude of places. This is one of the largest specimens known, nearly twelve inches in diameter, and was possibly made in Oxford c. 1340. Chaucer wrote an elementary treatise on the use of the astrolabe for his son, "lyte Lowis".

A brief document, possibly in Chaucer's own handwriting, arranging for a deputy to take over his Customs duties, presumably while Chaucer went abroad on the King's business.

Westminster Hall, was one of Chaucer's responsibilities as Clerk of the King's Works. The magnificent roof was completed in 1399 and has a span of 67 feet 6 inches, an architectural and engineering problem never before accomplished. The hall is part of the Palace of Westminster, better known now as the Houses of Parliament, and is used for great national ceremonies.

His life was by any standard rich and full. But it is of course as a poet and not as a public figure that he is remembered. Yet his remarkable achievement is certainly partly due to his wide experience of the world as well as to his acute powers of observation and his originality as a poet.

Chaucer's London was a walled city with a great church at its heart, very like this medieval artist's conception of Constantinople, and probably its citizens too enjoyed festivals where dancers wound their way out through the city gates to the sound of pipe and tabor.

Inside the city, streets would have been narrow, with overhanging upper floors. This street in Ledbury, Herefordshire, though later in date, gives an impression of what a medieval street was like.

THE LONDON he was born into was a compact city of forty thousand inhabitants squeezed into roughly one-and-a-half square miles. It was a maze of narrow, twisted and unlighted streets—only Cheapside was broad and straight—and the whole of London was contained in the area known as "the City" today. There were no pavements. People tried to walk near the crown of the street to avoid the filthy gutters, into which householders poured their slops, garbage and refuse. Shops were open-fronted, and like inns and public buildings had signs hanging outside to attract attention. Some streets looked like an almost continuous line of signs, and there were laws forbidding signs to project more than a certain distance. The houses, which were not numbered, were mostly of timber and plaster, with a stone one here and there. A few had gardens, and the Southwark shore of the Thames was green with trees. London Bridge was the only bridge. It had twenty arches, two chapels and a double row of houses. Above the tiled and thatched roofs of the city rose the wooden spires of a hundred churches. St. Paul's stood

Many trades were carried out in the street, and these knife-grinders and their wheel must have been a familiar sight.

on a hill and was easily the tallest. Westminster, with its abbey and Parliament, was two miles away, and Knightsbridge was a distant suburb. All round there were fields and pastures and thick forests full of deer and boars and even wild bulls. The countryside was very close. But inside the city walls there were noise and congestion. Medieval London, with its thriving port, its pageants and processions, its streets crowded with busy merchants, with shoppers and shouting tradesmen, must have been quite as noisy as London today. From his house in Aldgate in the eastern wall of the city Chaucer would have watched the traffic pouring in and out. At night the city gates were all closed, and people left the darkness of the unlighted streets for the quiet, if not the comfort, of their homes.

Homes were hardly comfortable by modern standards. Even the grandest of them, the castle, had little to offer as far as living conditions went. In Bodiam Castle in Sussex, which dates from the end of the fourteenth century, the arrangement of the Great Hall, with the solar (the private room of the lord and his family) at one end and the kitchen,

A royal carriage with a full load of noble ladies and pet animals.

Bodiam Castle, Sussex, with its great moat and causeway, was built at the end of the fourteenth century, both as a fortress and as an imposing dwelling for a noble family.

buttery and pantry at the other, is the same as in a private house of the period. The main differences are the extra private room and the large amount of space (about half) given over to defence. The wide moat crossed by a long causeway, the four huge circular drum towers at each corner, the six-foot thick walls, the two barbicans, two drawbridges and commodious barracks are a reminder that there was still a need for homes which were fortified strongholds.

In the manor house the usual position of the hall was on the ground floor, and the windows were low enough to give a view of the courtyard as well as more light and air. It was still the most important room in the house, less smoky and dirty than before, and most of the life of the place went on there. Previously the fire had been in the middle of the hall, with a hole in the roof as the only chimney. But splendid fireplaces were now being built, with tall chimneys in the thick walls. A small staircase led up to the solar, where the master of the house retired to be quiet or to go to bed. A window on the inner wall enabled him to look down into the hall. A wardrobe containing the family's

The manor house at Little Chesterford in Essex, a hall house where the fourteenth-century timbered hall forms the main part of the house with cross-wings at either end containing kitchens and bedrooms.

(Below) *A candlestick.*

clothes stood in the solar, and there were washing and lavatory arrangements. At the other end of the hall, under the minstrels' gallery, two doors led to the pantry, the buttery and the kitchen. Above the pantry and buttery was a spare bedroom for important guests. There were stables in the courtyard in front of the house, and a gatehouse opposite the porch. The whole building was surrounded by a moat or a wall.

The town house of the ordinary citizen was on a simpler scale. Built of timber and plaster, it had two storeys. Windows were seldom glazed, but had wooden shutters which were closed at night. A hall and bedroom were often the only living rooms; only the richer sort of house had a third room. The hall was grimy with soot, for there was no chimney, only a hole in the roof above the open hearth. In spite of the wooden seats with high backs, it must have been very draughty. No wonder furs were an important item of clothing. There was one bedroom for the whole household—including sometimes, as in *The Miller's Tale*, the lodger as well—and on occasions three occupants to a bed. At Wells choir school two smaller boys slept "with their heads to the head of the bed, and an older one with his head to the foot of the bed and his feet between the others' heads".

Not much is known about the cottages of the poor, as they have long ago disappeared. The poor widow's cottage in *The Nun's Priest's Tale* may have been built of logs, or perhaps thatched, the floor of bare earth, and with a yard enclosed by a fence and ditch. The life she led was very simple. Three cows, three pigs, a sheep—no doubt she sold the wool or wove it herself—and some poultry were all she had to keep herself and her two daughters. They lived on bread, milk, bacon and eggs. There was no money to spare for wine, fine sauces or any luxuries. In a bad year even the peasant farmer went short. In William Langland's *Piers Plowman* (written between about 1360 and 1399), a great allegorical poem with many striking pictures of medieval life, we read how Piers has neither eggs nor bacon, and no money to buy pullets or geese. Until next harvest all he has to feed his children are "two green cheeses, a few curds and cream and a cake of oats", some coarse bread and a few vegetables.

A bronze ewer, inscribed with the names "Tomas Elyot" and "Wyllem Elyot".

Even in the homes of the well-to-do, vegetables were less plentiful than they are today. There were peas, beans, cabbages and onions, but no potatoes and no swedes. Honey was used for sweetening, and cider and ale were the usual drinks. For flavouring meat (in winter and spring only salt meat was available) the cook depended on a variety of spiced sauces. In the Prologue to *The Canterbury Tales* we hear how the Franklin's cook was soon in trouble if his "sauces had no sting". This Franklin clearly had the means to gratify his taste for rich food:

> His bread and ale were both extremely fine,
> His cellars stocked with barrels of best wine,
> His larders too with many a tasty pie
> Of fish or meat, and in such rich supply
> His household seemed to snow with food and drink
> And every luxury a man could think.

A ploughman and his mate, warmly muffled against the cold weather, using a team of oxen to pull the plough.

The Abbot's Kitchen at Glastonbury, where elaborate feasts would have been prepared for the Abbot, who ranked as a great landowner, and for his noble guests.

The fishpond ensured a fresh supply of fish. It was a luxury that only the wealthiest could afford and was attached only to a manor house or perhaps a monastery. In the case of castles the moat was often used for this purpose too.

The Franklin's kitchen was probably an elaborate one by the standards of the times, though not as elaborate as a one-storeyed castle or abbey kitchen with a lantern or glazed dome at the top, with apertures to let out the steam and smell of cooking. A castle kitchen was a large, noisy and crowded place, with two or more open fireplaces and a large oven. Joints and poultry were roasted on spits in front of the open fire. The oven was built into the walls and had an iron door. To heat it, faggots were placed inside and lighted. When the brickwork was hot enough, the ashes were raked out and replaced by bread, cakes and pasties or meat pies. Once the oven had cooled down, its contents were ready for eating.

There were two meals in the day: dinner between nine and ten in the morning, and supper at five o'clock. They were served in the hall on trestle tables, which could be taken down afterwards and hung on the walls, and grace was said before and after each meal. Knives and spoons, often of beautiful design, were used, but not forks. Most people preferred to use their fingers. They threw the bones and scraps on to the rush-strewn floor for the dogs to fight for. When the rushes were filthy and began to smell,

Spoons—these are of cast tin—were, with knives, the only eating implements.

they were swept away and replaced with fresh ones. The dainty table manners of Chaucer's Prioress must have been most unusual:

> Her table manners were exceptional;
> No morsel from her lips did she let fall
> To drop upon her bosom, and of course
> She never dipped her fingers in the sauce.
> Her upper lip she always wiped so clean
> That on her cup no spot of grease was seen;
> She never grabbed a dish, but reached sedately;
> Her face was friendly and her bearing stately.

Furniture was scanty and strictly practical. The chest was the most important item. In a simple house there might be only one; it was about four feet long and it held linen,

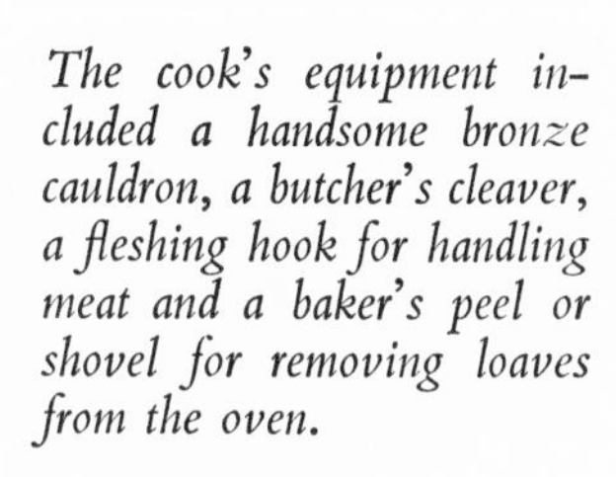

The cook's equipment included a handsome bronze cauldron, a butcher's cleaver, a fleshing hook for handling meat and a baker's peel or shovel for removing loaves from the oven.

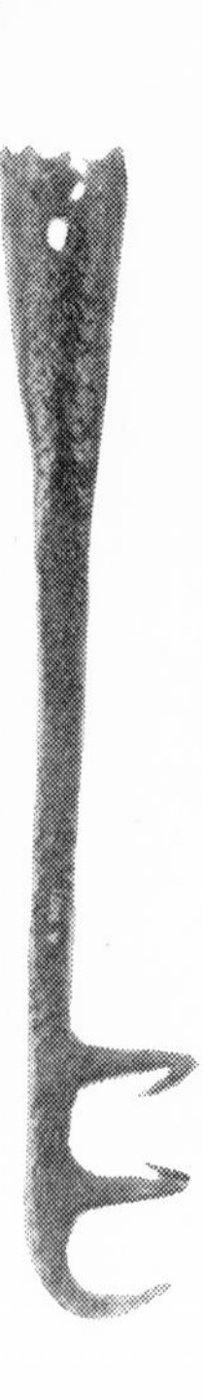

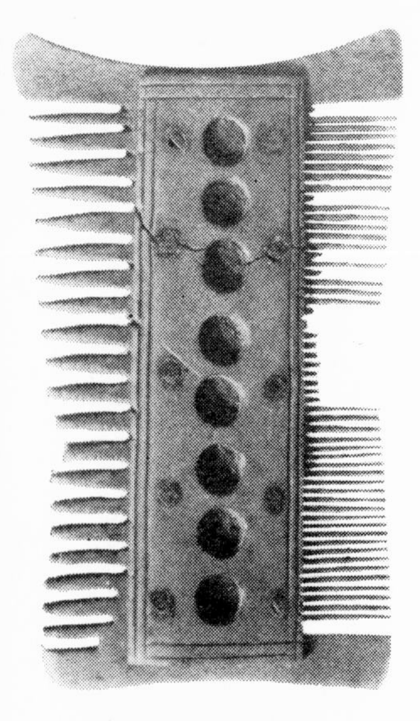

A comb of bronze and bone.

clothes and family possessions, as well as serving as a trunk on journeys. There were also chairs, benches, trestle tables and sometimes wardrobes for clothes. In style and appearance these were rather like church furniture. They had none of the lightness and grace that belong to later periods.

Fourteenth-century dress was rich in detail and elaborate. Though Chaucer himself, to judge from his portraits, dressed soberly in a long dark gown and plain hood, the young man of fashion was a striking figure.

An older man might wear a capuchon, or hood, and surcoat. The capuchon, which was worn until Tudor times, covered the whole head except for the face; the lower half was pulled down over the shoulders as a cape, and the upper half hung down at the back. Alternatively it could be worn as a sort of turban, folded and twisted above the crown. The Flemish beaver hat worn by the Merchant was fashionable for a time. The surcoat was a long, full-skirted gown, often made of brocaded material and lined with fur.

The lady also wore a surcoat. Underneath this her dress was full-skirted with a closely fitting bodice and a belt that rested on the hips. Her hair was carefully dressed and worn in plaits which were turned up to cover the ears. Sometimes it was worn in a golden net covering the whole head.

Enormous headdresses were popular with both sexes. Chaucer remarks that the kerchiefs that the Wife of Bath wore on her head on Sundays weighed a good ten pounds, while her hat was "as broad as is a buckler or a shield". Her tightly gartered hose, "of the finest scarlet red", were concealed under a flowing mantle.

Chests like this were used for holding possessions of all kinds—clothes, linen, documents and money—and, inevitably, for sitting on.

A young man of fashion—"Embroidered was he, as it were a meadow, All full of fresh flowers, white and red"—with his gay tightly belted tunic, carefully curled hair and elegant hose.

A half-boot of cowhide leather, the whole of the upper being cut in one piece and joined on the inner side with a single seam.

Two children's gowns with skirts made full by carefully inserted flared panels.

Traces of the medieval open field system are still visible at Laxton in Nottinghamshire.

THERE WAS no divorce between town and country such as we know today. Both the walled town and the open village were surrounded by unhedged fields, where every farmer cultivated his strip and grazed his sheep or cattle on the common pasture. At harvest time craftsmen from the town could by law be called upon to help. Most people were knowledgeable about country things, and Chaucer's imagery delights in the sights and sounds of the countryside.

The usual method of cultivation was the "open field". The arable land of the village was divided up into three or more fields and planted in rotation—one with oats or barley, one with wheat, while a third lay fallow. Peas, beans and rye were also grown. Each peasant-farmer had a number of strips to himself, divided fairly so that no one had more than his share of poor land. The strips were separated from each other by ditches, which acted as drains and carried off the water. The lord of the manor had legal rights over these peasants, who were really his serfs, or semi-bondsmen. On certain days of the year they had to work on his land instead of their own, under his bailiff's orders. The bailiff represented the interests of the lord, while the reeve represented those of the serfs. In the course of time he began to take over the functions of the bailiff. Chaucer's Reeve, for instance, enjoys the confidence of his lord even though he is clever enough to trick him on the sly, while the serfs fear him like the plague.

The Luttrell Psalter, produced between 1320 and 1340 for Sir Geoffrey Luttrell (d. 1345) of Irnham, Lincolnshire, has many detailed and most engaging drawings of agricultural work in progress. The oxen that drew the wooden ploughs were much smaller than they are today, for this was long before there was any knowledge of how to increase their size by scientific breeding. Horses also were smaller. Some of these drawings depict sowing and harrowing (the medieval harrow was much the same as ours), reaping with sickles under the lord's bailiff, feeding swine and herding cattle, taking corn to the lord's mill to be ground, stacking and threshing, penning sheep. The peasant, in his tunic, hood and breeches, seems to have been warmly clothed, but this was not everywhere the case. Langland in *Piers Plowman* writes of patched shoes and torn clothing, of children wrapped in rags and women walking barefoot on the ice.

During Chaucer's lifetime the old manorial system began to break down. Most peasants resented being taken off their own strips to work for the lord whenever he commanded. They came unwillingly, and bailiffs not unnaturally soon preferred hiring labourers who could work all the year round. Their wages were found in the rent which the lords now charged the peasants instead of requiring their services.

An event which hastened this change was the Black Death (1348–9), a deadly form of bubonic plague which wiped out a third or perhaps even a half of the country's inhabitants. With whole families destroyed, there were not enough labourers to till the land, and the few free labourers that were left demanded higher wages. Surviving serfs,

Coins: (top) *gold Guiennois struck by Edward the Black Prince at Bordeaux, 1363–72,* (middle) *florin of 1344 and* (bottom) *noble of 1360–9, all minted in Edward III's reign.*

Sheep were kept for milk as well as wool and meat. In this illustration from The Luttrell Psalter *one woman is milking a ewe, while others carry the milk away, possibly for cheese-making.*

A beggar woman with her child.

given derelict strips to cultivate as well as their own, were more resentful than ever of being dragged off to work for the lord. Sometimes they ran away to the other side of the forest to find work in other villages. With labour so short, they were unlikely to be turned away. The serf had another advantage too. Coinage might still be short, but with the population so drastically reduced there was now more to go round. It was no longer so difficult for him to save money, not only to pay rent for his strips but to buy his freedom too. And if he kept some sheep as well and sold the wool, as many now did, the necessary money would come all the more speedily. So serfdom began to disappear and the structure of society to change.

The Black Death was partly the cause of this change. Extremely contagious, it came originally from the East and was carried across Europe by black rats. In his introduction to the *Decameron*, Boccaccio describes it vividly, for it drove his story-tellers out of town to the country villa where they told each other the tales that make up the book. The plague returned again to England in 1361, 1362 and 1369. Dirt and lack of sanitation helped to spread it, and it was the towns and ports that were worst affected. In Bristol half the population died. Not only was agriculture badly hit, but economic, religious and artistic life was seriously disrupted too. Wages rocketed, and dead parish priests were hastily replaced by incumbents of far inferior quality. In building the highly skilled craftsmanship that had produced the English Decorated style was no longer available, and the simpler Perpendicular style took its place.

The plague is the background of *The Pardoner's Tale*. Three revellers are sitting drinking at a tavern when they hear a handbell clanging as a corpse is carried by. The tavern boy tells them that the dead man is one of their friends:

> There came a privy thief, they call him Death,
> Who kills us all round here, and in a breath
> He speared him through the heart, he never stirred.
> And then Death went away without a word.
> He's killed a thousand in the present plague,
> And, sir, it doesn't do to be too vague
> If you should meet him; you had best be wary.
> Be on your guard with such an adversary.
>
> (*translated by Nevill Coghill*)

Medical knowledge was not far enough advanced to cope with the plague, and outbreaks recurred at intervals till late in the seventeenth century, when the black rat was gradually expelled by the brown, which was not a carrier of the infection.

Illness was treated at home—not in hospital. A hospital was a refuge for the poor, without skilled provision for medical treatment. Most people had to make do with some homely remedy provided by a member of the family or a friend, as doctors were expen-

(Left) *Chaucer's Doctor of Physic, as he is shown in the Ellesmere Manuscript of* The Canterbury Tales, *carries as a sign of his profession the glass in which he examines the patient's specimens.* (Right) *A tooth-drawer at work.*

sive and only the rich could afford them. The Doctor in the Prologue was far from indifferent to money. He saved the gold which he earned during the outbreaks of plague, and he was in league with an apothecary able to provide him with patients as well as drugs—"each made money from the other's guile". Doubtless he took his fee from the patient before starting the cure, as this was the common practice. John Arderne, a well-known doctor of the day, wrote that the fee should never be less than five pounds (about £300 today, more than a year's wages for many people then). Disease was then thought to be caused by an excess of one of the four "humours"—phlegm, blood, yellow bile and black bile—the proportions of which in a man's body were believed to determine his temperament. Treatment consisted mainly of bleeding or purging. Chaucer praises the Doctor for his skill in diagnosis, as well as for his wide knowledge of ancient and medieval medical textbooks. He emphasises, too, that the medicine he prescribed had an astrological basis and must be administered only at the appropriate time—when planetary influences were most favourable to the patient. This was the teaching of the great Arabian doctors, who believed that the various parts of the body were controlled by different signs of the Zodiac. Orthodox medical opinion subscribed to this theory. So magic charms and effigies were regarded as powerful aids in effecting a cure in that superstitious age.

We hear of drugs and spices being imported from Venice—opium, senna, rhubarb, pepper and nutmeg—to be sold by apothecaries. Pepper was one of sixteen different

Girls married at an early age in the fourteenth century. The young bride in this picture is being betrothed to a decidedly middle-aged prince.

(Right) *Children often died young as the pathetic little tomb in Westminster Abbey of William of Westminster and Blanche de la Tour shows. They were two of Edward III's many children and died in 1340.*

remedies used for toothache. Henbane was some help in relieving pain. Powder made from burnt eel skins was blown up the nose to stop it bleeding. For smallpox John of Gaddesden, Court Doctor to Edward II, recommended wrapping the sick man in red cloths, and for diseases of the spleen the swallowing of seven heads of fat bats. Anaesthesia was unknown, but for an operation sleeping draughts made from a mixture of herbs were sometimes used. The surgeon was usually a barber or a quack until, in the middle of the fourteenth century, the master surgeons of London formed their own guild and the barbers' rough and ready attempts at surgery were thereafter restricted mainly to "bleeding".

Mortality amongst children, especially in infancy, was (not surprisingly) at a high rate. The babies of the better-off families were wrapped up very tightly in swaddling clothes like little Egyptian mummies and were usually given to wet-nurses to suckle, perhaps until they were three or four years old. Once they had left babyhood behind they were treated harshly, as if they were thoughtless and sinful adults who needed correction. The conception of children as faithful to their individual natures and developing gradually towards maturity did not exist. Their only playgrounds were the streets, and only a small proportion can have gone to school. In the country quite young children were required to help with jobs such as bird-scaring or driving oxen to the fields with goads. The brightest boys might, if they were lucky, learn their letters from the village priest. In towns and cities there were schools attached to churches and cathedrals. Here the choirboys learned to read and were instructed in the Christian faith. In the few grammar schools Latin was taught. "They made me learn Latin," wrote Jean Froissart (1337?–1410?), the French chronicler, of his own schooling, "and if I varied in repeating my lessons, they gave me the rod . . . I could not be at rest; I was beaten, and I beat in turn; then was I in such disarray that ofttimes I came home with torn clothes, when I was chidden and beaten again; but all their pains were utterly lost, for I took no heed thereof. When I saw my comrades pass down the street in front, I soon found an excuse to go and tumble with them again." Some French too was taught at the grammar school, also grammar, rhetoric (the art of speaking) and dialectic (the art of logical argument). A nobleman's son did not go to school, but had his own tutor.

There seems to have been little provision for the education of girls, and very few could have been able to read Latin. Sometimes they went as boarders to convents, to learn manners and deportment and perhaps a little reading. They were not sent to grammar schools, where the education was thought unsuitable for them. Girls were intended for marriage unless they went into a nunnery. So they stayed at home, where the nobly born learnt to cook and spin and sew, and the humbly born were also taught some craft or trade.

Spinning was a common occupation for women in all ranks of society. Here one woman is using a wheel, while another cards the wool to prepare it for spinning.

New College, Oxford, was "new" when it was established in 1379 by William of Wykeham, Bishop of Winchester, who also founded a school at Winchester with the intention of educating boys for the Church.

Because printing had not yet been invented, there were very few books, and none were graded to a child's age and interests. Chaucer himself, according to a statement in his *The Legend of Good Women*, owned sixty books, a very large number indeed at that time. They must have cost as much as eight or nine houses to buy. They would have been bulky, too, having been laboriously written by hand, probably on sheep or calf skin, then bound together with thick covers. Monks did most of the writing and copying. The ink was specially mixed, and pens were cut from goose quills. Few textbooks were available, and students acquired their knowledge mainly by sitting at the feet of a lecturer, taking down his words and learning them by heart. If a famous new teacher emerged, those who wished to learn from him had to go to his university to hear him. This meant travelling, sometimes to foreign parts, and indeed students or clerks made up a small but steady proportion of all travellers. Both in schools and universities education was largely a matter of oral instruction and learning by heart.

In England, Oxford and Cambridge were the only universities, and of these Oxford, thanks to the work of several generations of famous scholars and also to the influence of the religious reformer, John Wyclif, was at this period much the more important. The students came from grammar schools, though Chaucer himself did not go there. They were much the same age as modern undergraduates, though some went to the university when they were only fourteen. They were wretchedly poor and lived in halls or lodging houses, or occasionally, like Nicholas in *The Miller's Tale*, in a private home. The atmosphere was squalid and turbulent, and there were frequent riots between town and gown. The main faculties were those of theology, law and medicine. Those students intending to be priests or clerks—and they were the majority—generally remained for a year or two. They did not need to stay on to take a degree. But prolonged courses of study, lasting ten years or more, were usual for those with wider ambitions—seeking a position in the university or perhaps in the diplomatic service. The Clerk of Oxford in *The Canterbury Tales* was a student in training for a master's degree, scholarly, avid for learning, and sincere in his religious beliefs. With no spare cash for clothes or good food, he nevertheless refused to take a lay job, even though he had no income as yet from the Church.

Books were exceedingly valuable and so in libraries they were kept chained to their shelves, as in the library of Hereford Cathedral.

An ivory chessman of Chaucer's time found in London on the foreshore of the Thames.

AMONG RECREATIONS dancing both indoors and outdoors, in spite of the Church's disapproval, was popular with both sexes. In *The Franklin's Tale* Chaucer tells how a young wife, troubled by her husband's absence, is urged by her friends to forget her distress by dancing and playing chess and backgammon. In his *Description of London* William Fitzstephen, the author of an early life of Thomas à Becket, gives a vivid and exhilarating account of the relaxations of Londoners:

> In the holidays all the summer the youths are exercised in leaping, dancing, wrestling, casting the stone, and practising their shields; the maidens trip in their timbrels, and dance as long as they can well see. In winter, every holiday before dinner, the boars prepared for brawn are set to fight, or else bulls and bears are baited. When the great fen, or moor, which watereth the walls of the city on the north side, is frozen, many young men play upon the ice; some, striding as wide as they may, do slide swiftly; others make themselves seats of ice, as great as millstones; one sits down, many hand in hand draw him, and one slipping on a sudden, all fall down together; some tie bones to their feet and under their heels, and shoving themselves by a little piked staff, do slide as swiftly as a bird flieth in the air, or an arrow out of a cross-bow. Sometimes two run together with poles, and hitting one the other, either one or both do fall, not without hurt; some break their arms, some their legs, but youth desirous of glory in this sort exerciseth itself against the time of war.

Fitzstephen was writing in the twelfth century. Nevertheless John Stow, his translator, says that such forms of amusement remained popular till as late as the sixteenth

The popularity of chess is shown by the carving on this fourteenth-century ivory mirror-case.

Boys' games were rough and warlike and were a training for battle.

century. Boys much enjoyed playing at soldiers or the game of quintain. In this now forgotten game a pole, pivoted on an upright stake, had a shield fixed to one end and a bag of flour to the other. The player charged the shield with a lance. As he struck it, the bag of flour swung round and he had to dodge it. Another rough game played by boys and girls was "Hot Cockles". A blindfolded player, kneeling with his hands behind him, had to guess the name of any player who struck his hand. The blow was expected to be a hearty one aimed to knock him over. In the fourteenth century, due to the influence of the Church, which was always anxious to prevent feuding and disorders, laws were passed forbidding football, quoits and throwing the hammer in the fields near London. Archery, however, was widely encouraged. Wrestling was always popular, but in the country the commonest sport was poaching. In the absence of authorized recreations and outlets for youthful high spirits, it was also common among Oxford and Cambridge students.

Archers practising with the long-bow, the deadly weapon which won a string of battles for the English against the French.

The wool trade brought great wealth to the merchants who collected wool and shipped it to the Continent. William Grevel used his riches to build this splendid house at Chipping Campden in the Cotswold Hills. (Below) *The tomb of William Grevel and his wife.*

As England produced the best wool in Europe, it is not surprising that wool was the island's most important trade. There were far more sheep about than one ever sees today. The Sussex downs, the Cotswolds and the Yorkshire dales swarmed with them, and ordinary arable farms also had their flocks and shepherds. As well as the great sheep-farming lords and churchmen, peasants reared their own sheep. The wool for export was sent to Calais and paid for partly in cash, while bills were given for the rest. Most of it was raw wool, but during Chaucer's lifetime more and more woollen cloth was sent abroad. From the earliest times spinning had been the chief occupation of women at home, while weaving was done by websters, specially trained craftsmen who had looms set up in their cottages. The Cotswold village of Chipping Campden was one of the collecting centres. Here the beautiful stone house of William Grevel, one of the richest and most famous wool merchants of the day, is still to be seen in a fine state of preservation. Grevel was buried in the churchyard there in 1401. Chaucer's Merchant was probably a wool merchant, for one of his main concerns was to keep free from pirates the stretch of sea between Ipswich and Middleburg, both ports appointed to handle the export of wool. The cloth trade continued to increase in importance and finally to dominate the world's cloth market.

Like the wool trade, most industries were run by master craftsmen, and each had its own guild—the Tailors' Guild, the Goldsmiths' Guild, the Weavers' Guild, the Master Surgeons' Guild, and many others. These were the forerunners of the modern trades unions. They gave their members certain privileges, they fixed wages, laid down

working conditions and saw that honest prices were charged and sound materials used. The hallmark stamped on modern silver derives from this practice. They also helped widows and orphans as well as the sick—there is a record of the Carpenters' Guild giving fourteen pence a week to a member who was ill. Each guild was a powerful and closely knit unit of master craftsmen, apprentices and journeymen (men employed by the day). A boy apprentice would join when he was about fourteen, and his apprenticeship lasted seven years. He lived with his master and worked with him, he shared the same meals and at night he slept in the shop. But in Chaucer's day, as trade expanded, the gap between master and journeyman was already beginning to widen. The master had to give more and more of his time to organizing the business and selling the products. The seeds of capitalism had already been planted.

As trade and wealth increased, so the gap between rich and poor widened. The levying in 1380 of poll or head taxes was particularly hard on the poorest. This, together with general indignation against the governing class, resentment of the corruption and worldliness of the clergy, and hatred of repression, was enough to spark off the Peasants' Revolt in the following summer. Mobs of peasants from the counties round London marched upon the city, picking up others from the villages on their way. Thomas Walsingham, the fourteenth-century monastic chronicler, describes them as "the vilest of commons and peasants, some of whom had only cudgels, some rusty swords, some only axes, some bows that had hung so long in the smoke as to be browner than ancient ivory, with one arrow apiece, many whereof had but one wing. . . . Among a thousand such, you would scarce have found one man that wore armour." Their leader, Wat Tyler, was a man with unusual gifts of organization and discipline. He forbade all looting, and anyone who disobeyed was instantly beheaded. The London mobs opened the city gates to them, the Tower surrendered, and for nine days Wat Tyler was virtually ruler of England. After killing a number of unpopular figures such as Archbishop

Craftsmen in Chaucer's day had only simple tools to use. The carpenters who worked on the magnificent palaces and churches used an axe to shape the timbers they needed. Medieval pliers have a familiar shape, but a pair of tailor's shears looks unwieldy to a modern eye.

Sudbury, whose head was impaled on London Bridge, they met at Mile End the boy King Richard II, whose cool courage and reasonableness were to stave off catastrophe. The King agreed to their chief demands, including the abolition of serfdom, the poll tax and some trade restrictions, and also pardoned the rebels, all except their leader. In the dusk at Smithfield Wat Tyler was cut off from his men and beheaded by Mayor Walworth.

In *The Canterbury Tales* Chaucer takes as little notice of these stirring events as he does of the plague or the poverty of the masses. The only direct reference is in *The Nun's Priest's Tale*, where the farm labourers are chasing the fox:

> So hideous was the noise—God bless us all,
> Jack Straw and all his followers in their brawl
> Were never half so shrill, for all their noise,
> When they were murdering those Flemish boys,
> As that day's hue and cry upon the fox.
> (*translated by Nevill Coghill*)

Jack Straw was one of Wat Tyler's associates, and the Flemish boys were wealthy Flemish wool traders massacred by the mob in the general confusion.

A fifteenth-century artist drew this picture of two incidents in the Peasants' Revolt of 1381: on the left Wat Tyler is killed and on the right the young king, Richard II, courageously faces the mob.

Richard II, attended by richly dressed courtiers, receives a gift from a suppliant.

Such a revolt would hardly have been possible had some sort of police system existed. There was none at all. The nearest equivalent to a policeman was a sheriff, one of whose duties was to organize groups of men from the lower classes in "tithings" for holding local courts of law. He had to arrest suspects, keep them in prison while awaiting trial, and see that the decisions of the courts were carried out. The Robin Hood ballads bear witness to the common people's hatred of an oppressive and extortionate sheriff. The King too had little liking for him and suspected him of putting Crown funds into his own pocket. To keep a check on him and the local land-owners and their courts, a system of travelling justices touring the country in circuits had been devised by the Crown some two hundred years before Chaucer's day and was still in use. These travelling justices administered the King's law, and anyone who thought he had been wronged could take his case to them.

What of punishment? Two instruments of rough justice, the pillory and the ducking-stool, were common village features. But there was often no regularity about the administration of justice. An escaping thief or criminal who found sanctuary could not be touched. He had but to clutch the door-knocker of a church and he was safe from the processes of the law—but only for a time. Within forty days he had to go in sackcloth before a coroner and take an oath to leave the kingdom. This was called "abjuration of the realm", and he was not allowed long in which to go. In King Edward III's reign he had nine days to walk from Yorkshire to Dover. Judges could be bribed, so the rich and powerful could get away with anything; while murder committed even by the poorest was more commonly punished by "abjuration of the realm" than by hanging. Murder could even be excused or disregarded entirely. We hear of a reeve who, wanting to beat his mistress with a cudgel, killed the child in her arms by mistake, and the jury passed it off as an accident.

The real power was in the hands not of the King but of the nobles. The King lacked the resources to act against them, because it was they who raised, controlled and paid the bands of archers and professional soldiers, hiring them out for national service in time of war. As far as Parliament was concerned, the position was rather different. After meaning no more than "parleying" or discussion in the thirteenth century, the word was used officially to mean a full meeting of the King's Council—the greater and lesser nobles, clergy, and later on merchants—the King himself presiding. They did not come to legislate—legislation was devised by the judges and enacted by the King—but to hear what had already been decided. No wonder they came unwillingly, for it became their duty to enforce the King's decisions throughout the country. But in Chaucer's day there came a change. Arguing that if they were summoned to listen to the King and act for him, then they had the right to put forward their own petitions themselves, they appointed a Speaker at Westminster Hall to represent them and ask for what they wanted, whether it was an export duty on wool or the removal of an unpopular tax. For the first time counsellors came willingly, and with suggestions of their own to make.

In his old age King Edward's power was largely eclipsed by Chaucer's patron, John of Gaunt. When his influence waned and he retired to Spain, a group of rival barons, the Lords Appellant, were equally effective in preventing the young King Richard from governing. In the Merciless Parliament of 1388 the royal favourites were condemned, then executed or sent into exile. King Richard had to wait till 1397 to get his revenge on the barons and strip them of power. The period between John of Gaunt's dominance and Richard's revenge on the Lords Appellant was for Chaucer one of personal hardship and poverty, but to the long-drawn-out political struggle in the background he makes hardly any direct reference in his work.

A "forcer" or strongbox made of wood covered with leather and decorated with incised designs.

The medieval Church was exceedingly wealthy, its income being derived from its estates as well as from the taxes it received from the people. The Abbey of Tewkesbury built this handsome barn to house the produce the Church collected as tithes.

THERE WERE, however, two social movements which his poems, particularly the Prologue, reflect more positively. The first was the increasing importance of the middle classes. They are represented by two professional men—the efficient and learned Lawyer, a specialist in land purchase, and the shrewd and thrifty Doctor; also by the much travelled and smartly dressed wool Merchant, the prosperous and comfortably housed Franklin, the Guildsmen, and that expert weaver, the cheerful and much married Wife of Bath.

The other movement, one which he could hardly fail to reflect, was the general decline, through corruption and stiff conservatism, of the Church. In their anxiety for reform the Lollard heretics, the followers of John Wyclif, had already exposed it; so had the poets William Langland and John Gower. But the Church leaders took no heed. For the most part worldly, greedy, dishonest, overburdened with possessions—they owned something like a third of the land—they dug in their heels and refused to change. It was the period of the Great Schism (1378–1417), when the loyalties of Christendom were divided between two popes, one at Avignon recognized by the French, and the other at Rome, recognized by the English. The English bishops, capable and industrious though they might be, were more concerned with serving the State—they often went abroad on errands of diplomacy—than attending to diocesan affairs.

In the Prologue a good proportion of the pilgrims are connected with the Church: the Prioress, the Monk, the Friar, the Clerk of Oxford, the Nun's Priest, the Parson, the Summoner and the Pardoner. The Prioress was Lady Superior of a small convent, and

The "Crowned A", a pilgrim badge. Chaucer's Prioress wore one as a brooch, with the inscription "Amor vincit omnia" (Love conquers all).

responsible for the education of a few middle-class ladies. Chaucer's charming and gently ironical portrait suggests that she cannot have felt much religious vocation. She disregarded the Bishop's orders about how a nun's wimple should be worn, kept pets against the rules, wore a silver brooch with a sentimental inscription, and all in all had notably worldly tastes. More worldly still was that jolly and handsome *gourmet*, the Monk, with his liking for expensive furs and elaborate dishes, his love-knot and his passion for hunting the hare. And this was a man who, on entering his monastery, had taken vows of poverty, obedience and chastity. Not for him the contemplative seclusion of the cloister, or the strenuous manual work that St. Augustine's rule had imposed.

The friars were the great missionaries of the age. Their duty was to set an example of Christian living, doing good wherever they were needed, as well as to hear confession and to preach to an illiterate people who, in an age when books as well as education

A leather "costrel" or container for holy oil or water, carried home from shrines by pilgrims.

Monks singing one of the many services which marked the course of the monastic day.

Canterbury, to which Chaucer's pilgrims made their jovial way, was a major English shrine, and the city was crowded with inns, hostels for pilgrims, churches and religious houses. One such house was the Franciscan priory, Greyfriars, on the banks of the River Stour.

were scarce, never set eyes on a Bible. Chaucer's gossiping Friar Huberd was on the best of terms with wealthy squires and well-to-do women, a champion beggar and flatterer:

In every town
He knew the inns and taverns up and down.
To barmaids more than beggars he would come—
It didn't do to mix with common scum,
But with the rich. Where profit could be found,
Polite and humble he'd be hanging round.

The "Agnus Dei" or Lamb of God used as a pilgrim badge.

Summoners were petty officers of the Church, and their job was to bring to court adulterers, blasphemers and others who had broken ecclesiastical laws. Chaucer's Summoner was a buffoon who despised the Church, scoffed openly at all things sacred, and for a small tip would aid and abet his friends in their impiety. His friend the Pardoner, whose job was to sell indulgences, liberating sinners for a fee, had just come hot from Rome with his wallet stuffed with pardons. With his travelling exhibition of bogus relics—a pillow-case purporting to be Our Lady's veil, a glass full of pigs' bones, and so forth—he made more money than a country priest could in months of caring for his parish.

The friars were the great preachers of the Middle Ages and at their best were fervent missionaries. At their worst they were hypocritical rogues whom Chaucer and his fellow writers tried to expose.

The pilgrim badge of a cockleshell, the symbol of St. James of Compostella, whose shrine at Santiago de Compostela in Spain drew pilgrims (the Wife of Bath was one) from all over Europe.

The only churchmen with whom the poet is in sympathy are the Clerk of Oxford, who was in Holy Orders, and the poor Parson. The Parson, of lower social rank yet still a "clerk", an educated man, was clearly Chaucer's ideal parish priest. While many of his brother priests disappeared to London to earn an easy living as chaplains to trade guilds or singing masses for the souls of departed gentry, but still drawing the income from their parishes, this Parson stayed at home to look after his flock and practise what he preached:

> He was an active worker, generous, kind,
> And patient in adversity, you'd find.
> He loathed to excommunicate and curse
> Those who paid no tithes, but from his purse
> Freely he gave the poor his wherewithal;
> He lived on little, and his needs were small.
> Though wide his parish, the houses far asunder,
> Nor sickness nor misfortune, rain nor thunder
> Stopped his patient visits, staff in hand,
> To the lowest born or highest in the land.

Selflessness of this order must have been rare. The average peasant, uneducated, unable to understand the Latin words of the services, was doubtless acquainted with many Old Testament stories and knew something of the teachings of Jesus. But there was also a darker side to his religious thoughts. As G. M. Trevelyan, the social historian, observes: "fear of hell was a most potent force, pitilessly exploited by all preachers and confessors both to enrich the Church and to call sinners to repentance."

An early bombard. The use of artillery of this kind effectively changed fighting techniques, so that great castles and armoured knights became useless and new forms of warfare had to be developed.

THE HUNDRED Years' War was a constant background to Chaucer's life. It started in 1337 with King Edward III staking his claim to the French throne through his mother, Isabella, against King Philip VI of France. This long sporadic struggle, checked from time to time by the Black Death and never concluded by a general peace treaty, was more successful in its early stages. Edward's victory in 1346 at Crécy, where he was surprised by a much larger French army, ranks as one of the supreme achievements in the history of the British army. It was one of the first battles in which cannon were used, though they were at that time so small and unreliable that they seem to have been more noisy than effective. The victory was really due to the skill of the long-bow archers in breaking up the French cavalry squadrons ("they shot their arrows with such force and quickness," writes Froissart, "that it seemed as if it snowed,") after which the knights and men-at-arms dismounted and fought at the archers' side to finish the enemy off. Ten years later at Poitiers a repetition of this successful formula won for the Black Prince another resounding victory. The Black Prince (so called from the colour of his armour) was the eldest son of Edward III and a distinguished soldier. But the English lacked the money and resources to press home their advantage. By a treaty signed at Brétigny in 1360 Edward gave up his claim to the French throne, retaining only Calais, Ponthieu and Aquitaine. In his later years, as he grew senile and the Black Prince, worn out with campaigning, was taken mortally ill, the initiative went to France, now blessed with better generals and, in Charles V, a more resolute king.

The effigy of the Black Prince in full armour. From his tomb in Canterbury Cathedral.

The long-bow, the "mighty bow" which Chaucer's Yeoman carries, came originally from Wales and was adopted in the fourteenth century as the English national weapon. It had a considerable range, was more accurate and rapid in its rate of fire than the cross-bow which it replaced, and it could pierce armour. Until the early part of the fourteenth century armour had been simple, a shirt and leggings of mail and a steel helmet, with possibly plates of iron shaped to fit the arms and legs and to give additional protection. By the beginning of the fourteenth century knights were also wearing coats of plates, sleeveless coats sewn with pieces of iron, but this kind of armour proved defenceless against the long-bow. Something new was needed, and during Chaucer's lifetime armour as we generally think of it was developed: the armourers found a way of encasing the human body in close-fitting flexible plate. A knight still wore his mail shirt underneath and under that some sort of tunic. The one worn by Chaucer's Knight was made of coarse cloth which was stained with rust marks from his armour, for he had come straight from his foreign campaigns to join the pilgrimage.

Knights and squires would have been at their most splendid at jousts and tournaments, which were an essential part of knightly training. Their gay plumes and heraldry, the gorgeous caparisons of the horses, the elaborate tents and the gallery crowded with spectators, must have been a magnificent spectacle. The rules of these combats, in which the contestants aimed to unhorse each other, were stringent and surrounded with pomp and ceremony. Nevertheless the age of chivalry was by now really over,

(Above) *In battle a knight wore a helmet called a bascinet over a padded cap. The pointed visor could be removed. Beneath the armour a mail shirt was worn to protect parts of the body not covered by the plates.*

(Right) *The Black Prince's shield of poplar covered with canvas, plaster, paper and leather. At his death the shield, along with other pieces of his equipment, was hung above the prince's tomb.*

and the chivalric ideals represented by the Knight, with his gentle bearing, his reverence for truth, honesty and courtly behaviour, already had an old-fashioned flavour.

One of the campaigns in which the Knight had taken part was the siege of Algeciras in Spain in 1344, when it was taken from the Moorish king. In this age it was quite usual for knights to look for employment in foreign countries which were at war. Siegecraft was a carefully studied technique, and a variety of siege weapons was available. Once the besieging army had chosen the weakest part in the city walls for attack, a siege platform built to the correct height was moved forward for the attackers to swarm over. If there was a wide moat, it was usual first to fill part of it with earth, faggots and other debris to form a narrow and tightly packed bridgehead. This was done

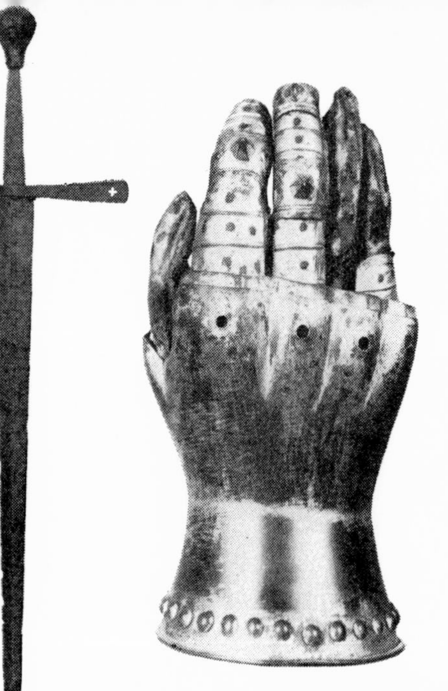

The Black Prince's gauntlet made of gilt-copper riveted to buff leather gloves which were embroidered with silk.

(Left) *Fourteenth-century swords were superb pieces of craftsmanship, easy to handle and perfectly balanced.*

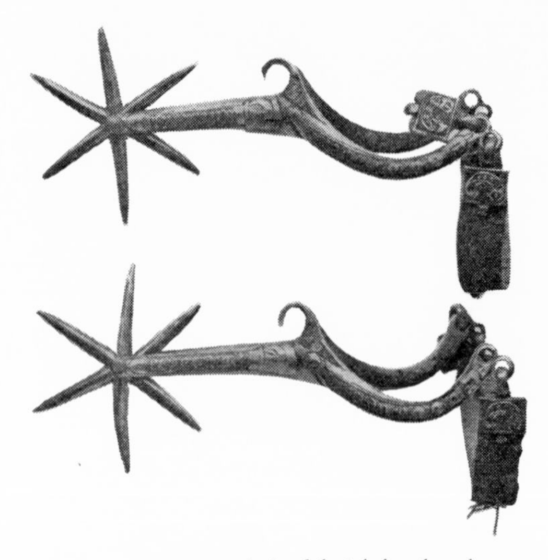

Spurs were a symbol of knighthood and so were often elaborately decorated.

War was in many ways a bloody and violent game, with a great element of pageantry and much talk of chivalry, but it was also an opportunity for looting on a grand scale.

The Black Prince's jupon, the quilted jacket, richly embroidered with his arms, which a knight wore over his armour.

under cover of the "cat", a movable shed with a sloping roof designed to throw off stones and boiling liquids dropped by the defenders. Then the "cat" was moved right up against the walls, and an iron-tipped battering ram slung under the roof and swung backwards and forwards to effect a breach. As medieval walls were normally only faced with stone and filled up in the middle with loose rubble, this was not as difficult to do as it sounds. When a large enough hole had been made, it was buttressed with props, then the besiegers fought their way through. Another way of forcing an entry, without recourse to the battering ram, was by means of a movable siege tower. The two scaffolding sides were hung with raw cattle hides to protect the soldiers, who swarmed up ladders to the floors inside, and eventually over the light wooden drawbridge lowered from the top on to the ramparts. Various weapons developed from the Roman catapult and ballista were available to help the besiegers. All sorts of things were used as ammunition—burning tar, horse carcasses, or even filthy refuse to spread diseases.

The nearest approximation to a navy was the fleet of small ships (by the end of Edward III's reign about twenty altogether) administered in London by the "clerk of the King's ships". Their main wartime use was for transporting soldiers and supplies. The typical fourteenth-century ship was tub-like in shape, with stem and stern raised and fitted out like castle turrets. There were cabins inside the castles, with ladders leading to the decks, a single mast surmounted with a crow's nest or fighting-top, a square sail, and a large hawse-hole for the anchor-cable. Rudders were beginning to take the place of steering-oars. Ships were used mostly for trading, but also for preventing piracy or French raids on the English coast. A sea-fight had no special and accepted tactics of its own, but was a glorified land battle on the water. The chief naval engagement during Chaucer's lifetime was Edward III's defeat of the French at Sluys in 1340. The numbers of the French were four to one against him, writes Froissart, and the engagement "fierce, murderous and horrible".

English gradually began to replace French as the language of literature and of the educated classes. The early work of the poet John Gower (1330?–1408) was written in French, but his *Confessio Amantis* (finished about 1390) was in English. William Langland's great allegorical poem *Piers Plowman* owed its form to the French, but in other respects—its mood, its theme, its Midland dialect, and its use of the alliterative metre derived from Anglo-Saxon—was thoroughly English. The other alliterative masterpiece of the period was the spirited and compelling *Sir Gawain and the Green Knight*, the work of an unknown poet. It may seem strange to us today that his contemporary Chaucer would have found the regional dialect of Cheshire and Lancashire, in which it was written, awkward and difficult to follow. The poem is very different in style and spirit

This delicately carved stone statue of the Virgin and Child is an outstanding example of fourteenth-century French Gothic art.

The simple structure of the ships which carried armies across the English Channel to war and took wool to Flemish looms, is shown on the seals of the Corporations of the Channel ports of Dover and Winchelsea.

A handsome example of the goldsmith's skill, the Gold Cup of the Kings of England and France.

from *The Canterbury Tales.* Steeped as he was in French and Italian literature, linguistically Chaucer's great achievement was that he wrote from the beginning in the English of London, transmuting it with his genius and creating the moulds which were to shape throughout the centuries to come some of the greatest poetry in the world. Chaucer's English is not difficult to read, although at first glance some of the words seem strange, as this passage from *The Reeve's Tale* shows. John and Alan, two students from Cambridge, suspect the miller at Trumpington of cheating them and resolve to watch the milling operations very closely, but the wily miller distracts their attention by setting their horses loose.

And whan the mele is sakked and ybounde
This John goth out and fynt his hors away,
And gan to crie "Harrow!" and "Weylaway!
Oure hors is lorn, Alayn, for Goddes banes,
Step on thy feet! Com out, man, al atanes!
Allas, our wardeyn has his palfrey lorn."
This Aleyn al forgat, both mele and corn;
Al was out of his mynde his housbondrie.
"What, whilk wey is he geen?" he gan to crie.
The wyf lepynge inward with a ren.
She seyde, "Allas! youre hors goth to the fen
With wilde mares, as fast as he may go.
Unthank come on his hand that boond hym so,
And he that bettre sholde han knyt the reyne!"

Here is a literal translation:

And when the meal was sacked and bound,
John went out and found his horse had gone,
And began to cry "Help!" and "Alas!
Our horse is lost, Alan. God's bones, man,
Use your legs! Come out at once!
Alas, our warden has lost his palfrey!"
Alan forgot everything, both meal and corn;
All idea of prudence went right out of his head.
"What's that? Which way has he gone?" he cried.
The (miller's) wife came leaping and running towards them.
"Alas!" she said. "Your horse has gone to the fen
After the wild mares as fast as he can go.
Curse the hand that tied him so (carelessly)!
The man should have known better how to knot the reins."

The choir of Gloucester Cathedral which typifies the Perpendicular style. The East Window is a memorial to those who fell at Crécy.

From the Italians Chaucer took over the four and five-beat syllabic verse line, adapting it to suit his purposes, and using it with great delicacy and variety. He used other metres too, but the five-beat rhymed couplet has remained a favourite for English verse ever since. There were other ways too in which he was a great innovator. He extended the range of medieval poetry to include dramatic story-telling (*Troilus and Criseyde* is almost like a novel) and deft characterization, and no other English poet of his stature can rival him for humour—farcical, scurrilous, satirical, witty and urbane, he is a master of each sort. But perhaps the most original thing about him was his attitude to human life; "large, free, simple, clear, yet kindly", Matthew Arnold, the nineteenth-century poet and critic, calls it, for the poet had "the power to survey the world from a central, a truly human point of view".

In his day it was the educated classes who read Chaucer. The illiterate were reached by another branch of literature, the Mystery Plays. These were performed by the guilds

A portative organ.

on stages with wheels. Written in rhyming stanzas, they taught versions of the Bible stories from the Creation, through some of the chief events of the Old and New Testaments, to the Last Judgement. The Chester, York and Coventry Cycles of plays all belong to this period.

In architecture the age saw the adoption of the Perpendicular style. A fine example is the choir of Gloucester Cathedral. In the visual arts there were new developments in stained glass and in painting, while in sculpture effigies and tomb carvings had great richness of detail. In music the century was less creative than its predecessor, but Chaucer's poetry shows clearly what an important feature it was of medieval life. The melody of the hymn "Angelus ad Virginem" which, in *The Miller's Tale*, the lecherous young gallant Nicholas sang at night, was a popular late fourteenth-century setting. He accompanied himself on the psaltery, a sort of shallow harplike instrument, with strings stretched across, and rather like a dulcimer. The main difference was that the psaltery was plucked by the fingers, while the dulcimer was played with little hammers. The bagpipe, played by the Miller as he brought the pilgrims out of town, appears from the portrait in the Ellesmere manuscript to have had only one drone. In the shape of the bag and in the fingering it is the same as the modern Scottish bagpipe. The organ was common in churches, but must have been smaller in size and less solemn in tone than its modern counterpart. Like the bagpipe, it was a *merry* instrument. "His voice was merrier than the merry organ," says Chaucer of the cock Chanticleer in *The Nun's Priest's Tale*. Organ playing was called "organ-thumping": in 1308 we hear of a musician being paid "to thump the organs and teach the choirboys, and instruct any of the monks who wish to learn the art of organ-thumping". Other instruments of the period were the harp, the viol and the shawm—a forerunner of the oboe. Outdoor dancing was accompanied by pipe and tabor, and horns and trumpets were used in hunting. The country abounded with professional minstrels, some of them permanently

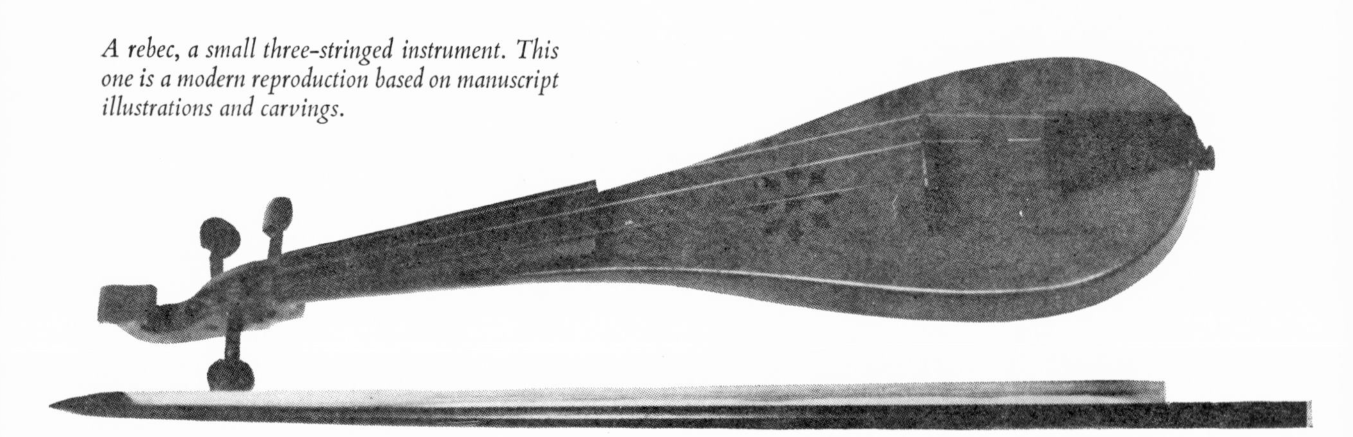

A rebec, a small three-stringed instrument. This one is a modern reproduction based on manuscript illustrations and carvings.

(Right) *Chaucer reading to Richard II and his court. This beautifully illuminated page forms the frontispiece to one of the best manuscripts of Chaucer's poem* Troilus and Criseyde.

attached to a lord's household, others wandering far afield and able to contribute all kinds of entertainment, sometimes including tumbling and dancing.

It was a virile and adventurous age, with new ideas stirring, new forms of society establishing themselves, new weapons and techniques. With the growth of overseas trade and the increase in wealth, a new merchant class arose to counterbalance the power of the Church and the old nobility. As Anglo-Norman French gave place to the English of London, which now became the standard language, the country awoke to a new sense of nationhood. The material conditions of life were for most people considerably harder than they are today. In an age of ill-controlled lawlessness and disease, much energy and ingenuity were needed for survival. And yet against this sombre background literary and artistic achievement stood out brilliantly, with Chaucer himself firmly in the centre of the picture. Though he seldom referred directly to contemporary events, the pilgrims in the Prologue to *The Canterbury Tales* came straight from his day and age. Himself a man of the world, shrewd, easy-going, with a vivid imagination and a fund of robust humour, he created them out of the abundant variety of life around him. But they also belong to all time. At this distance they may appear to have strange habits, outmoded beliefs, and peculiar clothes, yet they are still convincing proof that human nature itself has changed very little through the centuries.

The portrait of Chaucer which appears in the Ellesmere Manuscript of The Canterbury Tales. *The poet, with his pen-case fastened to a button on his coat, is obviously deep in the telling of a tale, perhaps one of the two he impishly plagued his fellow pilgrims with, the jog-trot parody of knightly adventure,* Sir Thopas *or the prose tale of* Melibee.

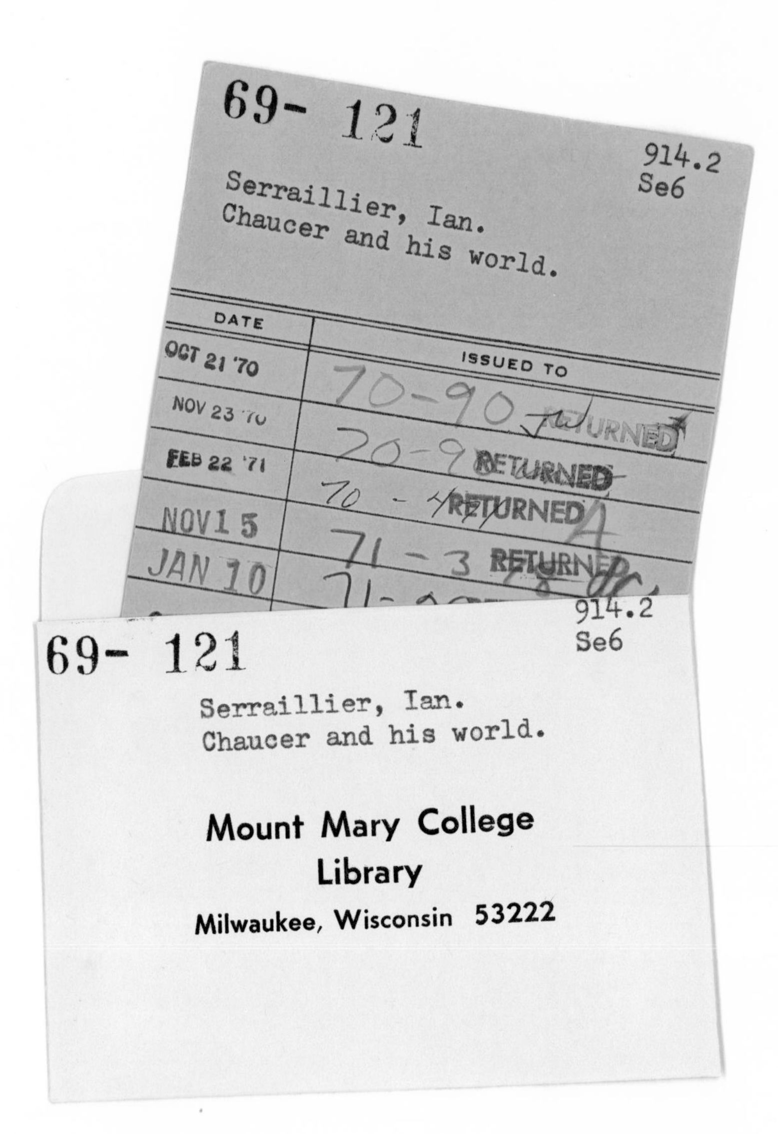

69- 121
914.2
Se6
Serraillier, Ian.
Chaucer and his world.
DATE
ISSUED TO
OCT 21 '70
70-90
RETURNED
NOV 23 '70
RETURNED
FEB 22 '71
RETURNED
NOV 15
RETURNED
JAN 10
RETURNED
914.2
Se6
69- 121
Serraillier, Ian.
Chaucer and his world.
Mount Mary College
Library
Milwaukee, Wisconsin 53222